The Official United States Olympic Committee

Curriculum Guide
to the Olympic Games

The Olympic Dream

PRIMARY

Griffin Publishing Group
Glendale, California

The Olympic Dream

10 9 8 7 6 5 4 3 2

ISBN 1-58000-014-2

This publication is the result of many talented and devoted supporters of the Olympic Games from
Griffin Publishing and Teacher Created Materials, Inc.

PUBLISHER	Griffin Publishing	CO-PUBLISHER	Teacher Created Materials
PRESIDENT	Robert M. Howland	EDITOR	Evan D. Forbes, M.S.Ed.
COORDINATOR	Robin L. Howland	WRITER	Cindy Holzschuher
COVER DESIGNER	Chris Macabitas	ILLUSTRATOR	Phil Hopkins

U.S. Olympic Committee

William J. Hybl	President
Richard D. Shultz	Executive Director
John Krimsky, Jr.	Deputy Secrectary General
Barry King	Director, Marketing/Fund Raising Communications
Mike Moran	Director, Public Information & Media Relations
Sheila Walker	Education Programs

Griffin Publishing Group
544 W. Colorado Street
Glendale, CA 91204
Phone (818) 244-1470 / Fax (818) 244-7408

U.S. Olympic Committee
One Olympic Plaza
Colorado Springs, CO 80909
Phone (719) 632-5551

Manufactured in the United States of America

Table of Contents

Introduction

Every two years there is a special excitement in the air. The eyes and ears of the world are on athletes who meet in friendly competition to see who is the fastest runner, the highest jumper, the speediest skier, the most graceful skater. Top athletes from around the world compete for medals signifying that they are the best. This book is about the Olympic competition and covers both Summer Olympic Games and Winter Olympic Games. It includes ideas, materials, and activities that can be used with students in primary grades.

The contents are designed to provide the following:

- Information and practice activities to familiarize students with the Olympic Games
- Creative worksheets to challenge students to recall and apply what they have learned
- A complete game to bring the spirit of the Olympic Games to your classroom
- Plans for a Mini-Olympics culminating activity
- Suggestions for additional activities and enrichment
- Teacher resources including bulletin board, learning center(s), answer key, art patterns, and bibliography

These materials are appropriate for the following:

- Class or group lessons
- Independent enrichment and research
- Cooperative learning activities

The Olympic Summer Games, usually held in July or August when many students are on vacation, may be introduced to them at the end of the traditional school year. Thus, they can better appreciate the Games on television or in person.

The Olympic Winter Games, held in January or February when most schools are in session, offer the opportunity for additional activities based on the daily schedule of the Games.

The hope for peace is renewed at the Olympic Games. When the Olympic flag is flying and the Olympic flame is burning, we think of world peace and cooperation. As we watch the ceremonies and competitions, we appreciate and respect the talent and dedication of individual athletes. Differences in nationalities fade as similarities in human spirit emerge. We hope this book will bring the Olympic spirit alive for you and your students.

Bulletin Board

You can easily create an effective bulletin board display using the pictograms on pages 72–76. Cover the board with white paper. Cut apart the pictures and glue each one to a 6" (15 cm) square of red, green, blue, or yellow construction paper. Print the words "The Olympics" in large letters across the top center of the bulletin board. Ask students to trace, color, and cut five circles (one each in red, green, blue, yellow, and black) to glue in place as the Olympic rings. Add the labels "Winter" and "Summer" on either side of the board under the title heading. Attach the pictograms under the correct heading.

As the unit progresses, use the bulletin board to display appropriate student work and sports pictures from print media.

Learning Center(s)

Class Lessons

You will probably teach the Olympics as a social studies unit. Try to devote some time each day to the unit. It is not necessary to use each page in this book, nor must every student complete every activity. Make your assignments appropriate to the needs of the individuals in your class. You can use your creativity to extend the theme across the curriculum by using the additional suggestions on pages 70 and 71.

Center Approach

You can create a simple center with enrichment or art projects for the Olympic unit. The center can provide worksheets or manipulative activities for students who need remediation. Use the information in this unit to create and adapt materials that directly address your curricular needs.

The center should have a small bulletin (or peg) board to display a colorful logo and directions. There must be a table large enough for two or three students, art supplies, and research materials. Here are some task ideas to help you begin:

–Locate five different national flags in an encyclopedia and color them correctly.

–Cut five flags and glue them correctly on the map of the world.

–Cut and paste the Summer or Winter Games Jigsaws (pages 30–35).

–Design a poster for the next Olympic Games, showing the city and dates.

–Read about the host city. Make a list of five landmarks.

–Read a book about an Olympic athlete. Then write five facts about that person.

–Write two word problems using numbers related to a sport.

–Write/draw pages about your favorite Olympic sport to be combined in a class book.

–Play the Road to the Olympics Game (pages 59–63) with a friend.

–Classify a list of athletes according to their sport.

–Draw a symbol (or piece of equipment) to represent five different sports and then label them.

–Write three good menus for an athlete in training.

–Create a crown of olive leaves from paper and pipe cleaners.

Where Do You Fit In?

People all over the world have favorite sports and favorite athletes. What are your favorite sports? Who are your favorite athletes?

Sports I Like to Play	Sports I Like to Watch	Is It an Olympic Sport?

My Favorite Athletes	Sports They Play	Have They Ever Been in the Olympic Games?

You are about to begin learning about the Olympic Games.

Here are some things you can do to get started:

- Make a list of Olympic sports.
- Learn the dates and locations of the next Winter and Summer Games.
- Listen to news reports on television about the upcoming Games. Share what you hear with your class.
- Cut out newspaper and magazine articles about the upcoming Games. Share your information with your class.

Ancient Greece

The Olympics started in the Valley of Olympia in 776 B.C. The Games lasted five days and were only for men and boys.

The first day was spent getting ready to compete. The athletes chose their best games. The judges promised to be fair.

On the second day there was a chariot race. A chariot is a two-wheeled carriage pulled by four horses. Athletes also ran foot races and did long jumps on this day.

On the third day there was a big feast. Later there were foot races, boxing, and wrestling for boys.

The fourth day was for men's foot races, boxing, and wrestling. Some of these events were very rough. Some men got hurt.

On the fifth day the winners were given crowns of olive leaves.

What do the following words mean?

ancient _____

athlete _____

chariot _____

compete _____

feast _____

How do you think the Olympics got its name?

_____

_____

_____

_____

_____

_____

Ancient Greece Recall

Directions: Make a picture to show what happened each day of the Olympics in ancient Greece. Cut apart the pages and make a book.

ANCIENT GREEK OLYMPICS	**Day 1**
Day 2	**Day 3**
Day 4	**Day 5**

Modern Games

Baron Pierre de Coubertin is the father of the modern Olympic Games. He thought the new Games would be a good way for people of different races to understand each other.

The first modern Olympics were held in Athens, Greece, in 1896. Athletes came from ten countries. The United States sent the largest team and won the most gold medals.

There were no Olympic Games during World War I and World War II.

Today, there are Winter or Summer Games every two years. Almost 200 countries send athletes to participate, in hopes of winning gold, silver, or bronze medals.

Directions: Circle the words in the story above that answer these questions.

1. Who is the father of the modern Olympic Games?
2. Where and when was the first modern Olympic Games held?
3. Which country sent the largest team?
4. How many countries send athletes to the Olympics today?
5. What materials are used to make the Olympic medals?

Why do you think there were no Olympic Games during World War I and World War II?

_____

_____

_____

_____

_____

_____

_____

Modern Games Sort

Directions: Write the event on the line under the correct sport description. Some events may be used more than once.

Winter	Summer
bobsled	baseball
figure skating	basketball
ice hockey	cycling
luge	diving
skiing	soccer
speed skating	swimming
	track/field

Sports in Water

_____

_____

Sports Using a Ball

_____

_____

_____

Sports on Ice/Snow

_____

_____

_____

_____

_____

_____

Sports on a Track

_____

_____

_____

Ancient and Modern Games

Use the Venn diagram to show the similarities and differences between the ancient and modern Games.

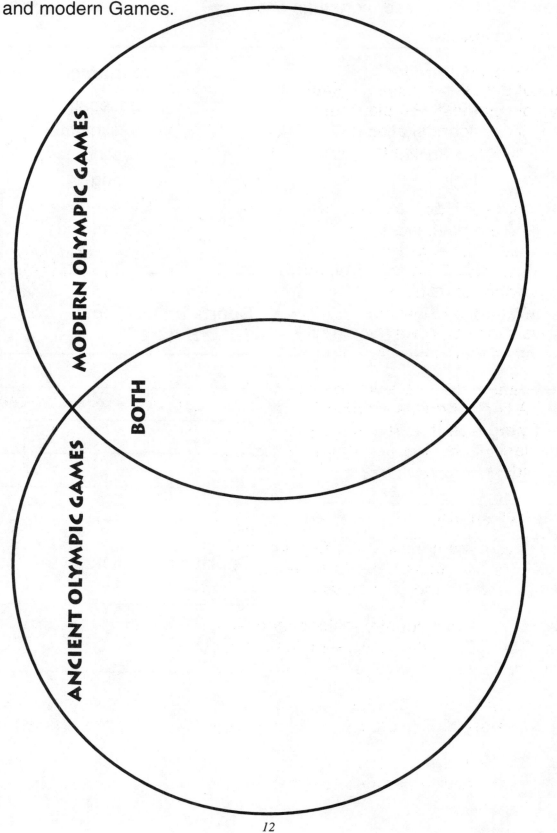

Opening and Closing Ceremonies

Opening Ceremonies

Each host city plans a special program of dance and music to start the Olympic Games. People from the host city perform together to welcome visitors from around the world.

Athletes from each country parade into the stadium. Members of the team choose an athlete to carry their nation's flag. The Greek athletes are given the honor of leading the parade. All others follow in alphabetical order. However, the host country's team is always last.

After the parade there is a welcoming speech. A flock of doves—birds of peace—fly over the stadium and the Olympic flame is lit. The ceremony usually ends with fireworks.

Closing Ceremonies

After 16 days of competition, the Olympic athletes gather in the stadium to say goodbye. Many of them have new friends from other countries. They are proud of their medals and their native lands.

People from the host country make speeches about what happened at the Games. The flag for the next Olympic host country is raised and people from that country invite everyone to attend the next Olympic Games.

The Games are closed and the flame is put out. The Olympic flag is taken down. There are music, dancing, and fireworks at the end of the ceremony.

Activity: Make a drawing of a scene from the opening or closing ceremonies on the back of this or a separate piece of paper.

Olympic Card Trick

Sometimes at the opening ceremony of the Olympics, there are colored cards taped to the seats. The people hold up the cards, and they fit together to make a picture or message.

Directions: Color the card trick below.

   1—blue   2—black   3—red   4—green

Leave the squares with no numbers uncolored.

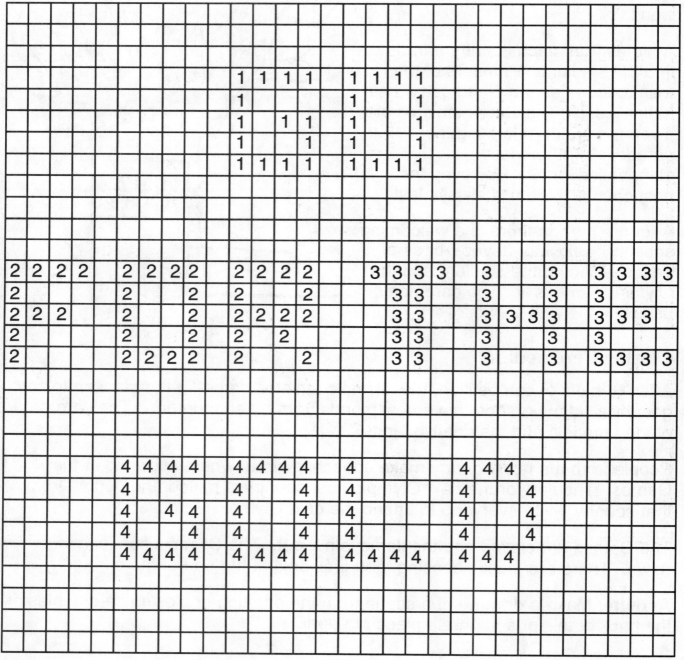

The Olympic Symbol

Baron de Coubertin, who helped initiate the modern Olympics, used the rings to symbolize the five continents of the world. These probably included North and South America (counted as one), Europe, Asia, Africa, and Australia. He chose the colors blue, yellow, black, green, and red because the flag of each competing nation has at least one of these colors.

The colored rings placed on a background of white became the design for the Olympic flag. Although displayed at Paris, France, a few years before, it was first flown at the Olympic Games in Antwerp, Belgium, in 1920. Since then it has been raised at the opening ceremonies of each successive Olympics.

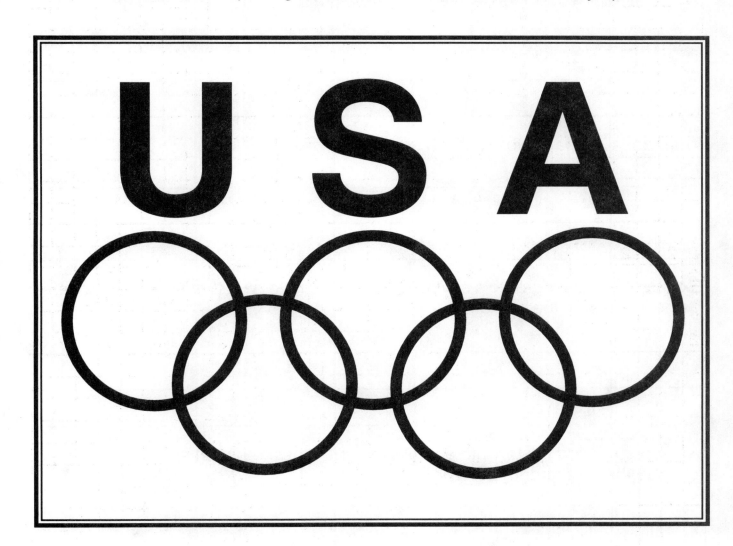

The Olympic Oath

At the opening ceremonies for the Olympics, an athlete from the host country leads all the other athletes in saying the Olympic oath. An oath is a declaration or promise. An Olympic oath is a promise to play fairly.

Here are the words of the oath:

In the name of all competitors, I promise that we shall take part in these Olympic Games, respecting and abiding by the rules which govern them, in the true spirit of sportsmanship, for the glory of the sport, and the honor of our teams.

Why is it important to follow the rules of a sport?

_____

_____

_____

What does it mean to be a "good sport"?

_____

_____

_____

Explain the meaning of this saying: "It doesn't matter whether you win or lose; it's how you play the game."

_____

_____

_____

Work in small groups to write an oath for your class to use at sporting events or to guide their classroom behavior.

_____

_____

_____

The Olympic Torch

Before the start of the Olympic Games, a flaming torch is carried from Athens, Greece, to the host city. It may ride in a boat or on a plane. Runners carry the torch across the host country to the Games.

Directions: Color the flame. Print the city and country of the next Olympic Games on the writing lines provided on the front of the torch.

Design an Olympic Pin

Special pins are made to wear at the Olympic Games. People like to collect these pins. The pins can show the Olympic symbol, mascot, logo, etc.

Directions: Design three pins that could be sold at the next Olympic Games.

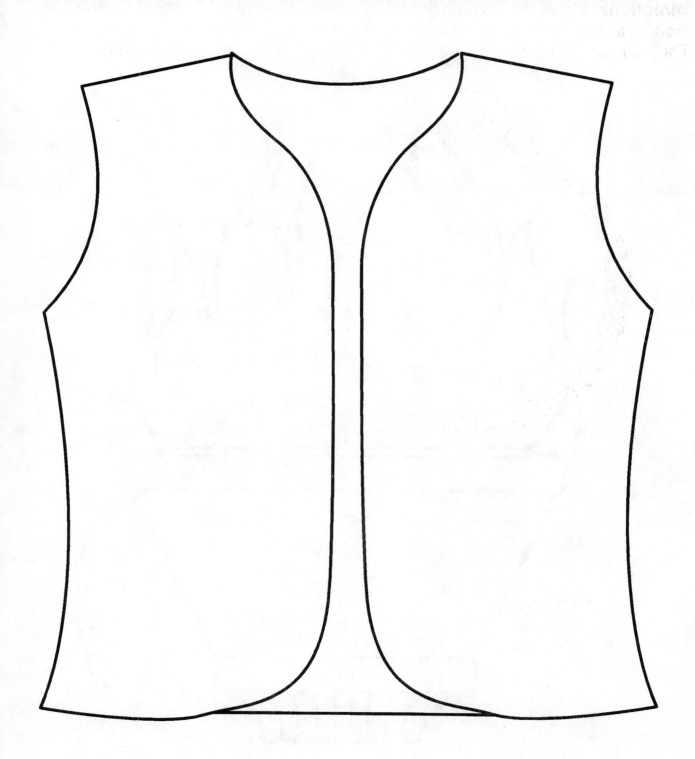

Olympic Medals

The first Olympians won crowns of olive leaves. Today winners receive gold, silver, or bronze medals. It is an honor just to be in the Olympic Games. Not everyone is able to win a medal.

Directions: Make three copies of the medal pattern on this page. Cut out and create a design for gold, silver, and bronze medals for the next Olympic Games. They should show the name of the host city and the year of the Games.

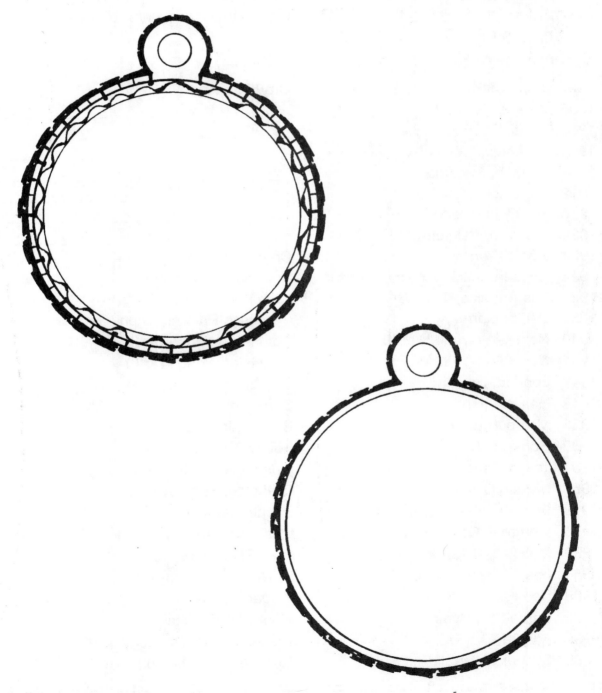

Host Cities

On the following pages (21–23) you will find the flags of Olympic host countries where U.S. athletes have competed.

- Use a reference book to find the flags and name the countries.
- Color the flags and cut them out.
- Sort them into two piles: flags that flew over the Winter Games and flags that flew over the Summer Games.
- Match the flags to the countries on a map of the world (pages 69–70).

Summer	**Winter**
Year City/Country	**City/Country**
1896 Athens, Greece	_____
1900 Paris, France	_____
1904 St. Louis, MO, USA	_____
1908 London, England	_____
1912 Stockholm, Sweden	_____
1916 Not Held (World War I)	_____
1920 Antwerp, Belgium	_____
1924 Paris, France	Chamonix, France
1928 Amsterdam, The Netherlands	St. Moritz, Switzerland
1932 Los Angeles, CA, USA	Lake Placid, NY, USA
1936 Berlin, Germany	Garmisch-Partenkirchen, Germany
1940 Not Held (World War II)	Not Held (World War II)
1944 Not Held (World War II)	Not Held (World War II)
1948 London, England	St. Moritz, Switzerland
1952 Helsinki, Finland	Oslo, Norway
1956 Melbourne, Australia	Cortina, Italy
1960 Rome, Italy	Squaw Valley, CA, USA
1964 Tokyo, Japan	Innsbruck, Austria
1968 Mexico City, Mexico	Grenoble, France
1972 Munich, West Germany	Sapporo, Japan
1976 Montreal, Canada	Innsbruck, Austria
1980 Moscow, USSR	Lake Placid, NY, USA
1984 Los Angeles, CA, USA	Sarajevo, Yugoslavia
1988 Seoul, South Korea	Calgary, Canada
1992 Barcelona, Spain	Albertville, France
1996 Atlanta, GA, USA	1994 Lillehammer, Norway
2000 Sydney, Australia	1998 Nagano, Japan

Flags

Olympic Winter Games

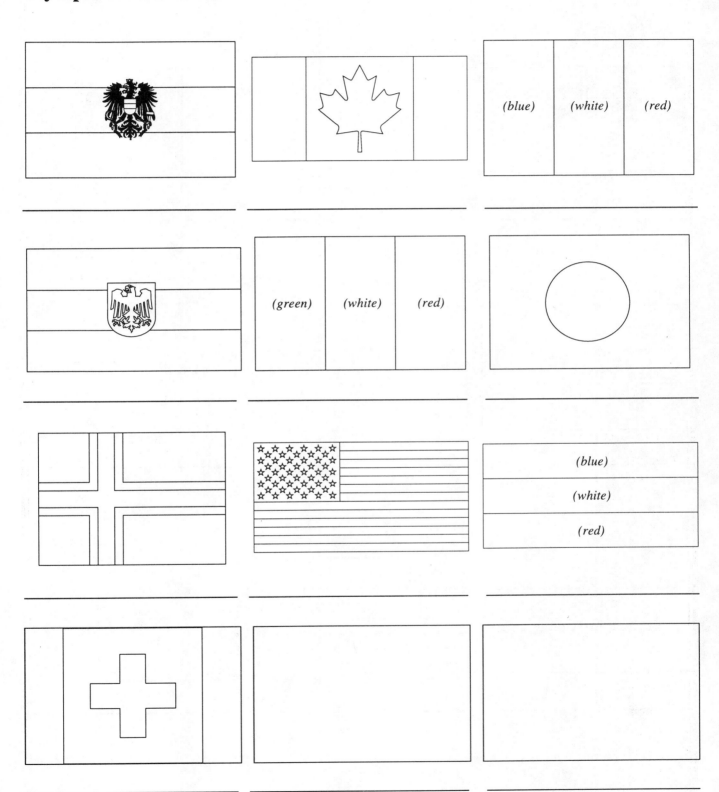

Flags *(cont.)*

Olympic Summer Games

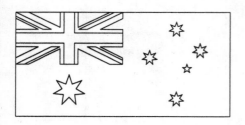

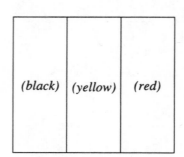
(black) (yellow) (red)

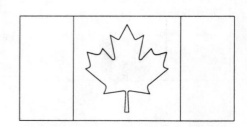

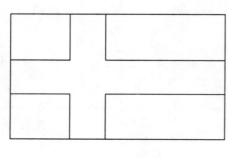

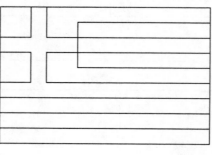
(blue) (white) (red)

(green) (white) (red)

Flags *(cont.)*

Olympic Summer Games

Design a Logo

Every Olympic Games has its own logo. The logo is not the same as the symbol with five rings.

Below is the logo of the ancient Games. It shows a discus thrower. He stands for the strength and power of all Olympic athletes.

Here are some logos from modern Olympic Games.

Activity: Pretend your city might host the Olympics some day. Draw a logo that shows the name of your city, the year, and a small picture. If you wish, include the five Olympic rings.

Design an Olympic T-Shirt

Directions: Add an Olympic logo or symbol to this T-shirt.

Design a Mascot

The host city decides on a mascot to advertise the Olympic Games. It is usually a small animal or bird like a raccoon, bear cub, tiger cub, eagle, etc.

The first mascot was a small dog named Waldi. His head and tail were blue. His body had red, green, and yellow stripes.

Directions: Draw your own mascot holding an Olympic flag.

Design a Poster

Directions: Suppose the Olympic Games were coming to your city. Draw a poster that shows the name of your city, the year of the Games, and the Olympic logo or symbol.

The Olympic Site

Map Skills

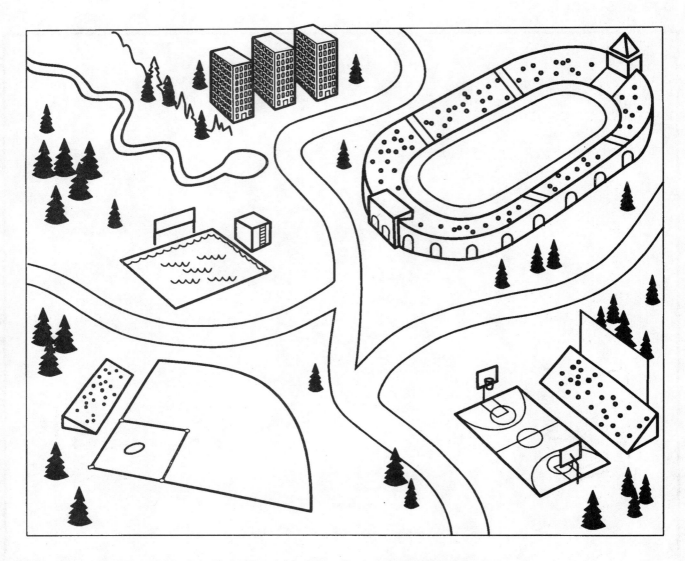

Directions: Read the following information and do what it says.

1. Add an Olympic flag to the top of the stadium.
2. Draw a baseball bat and glove on the field.
3. Draw a basketball on the arena sign.
4. Circle the building(s) where the athletes live.
5. Draw a mountain bike at the top of a slalom course.
6. Draw a pair of running shoes on the track.
7. Draw a diving board at the pool.

Site Report Form

Visitors to the Olympics often want to tour the host city. You will enjoy your visit more if you have some information before you begin.

Directions: Use a reference book to find the answers about the host city of your choice.

City _____ Country _____

Here are some interesting things to see and do:

Museums: _____

Entertainment: _____

Landmarks: _____

Shopping: _____

*Design a travel brochure for the city you have chosen. Fold a paper in half lengthwise. Make a drawing on the front and print the information inside. On the back, print some "Fast Facts" about the Olympics.

To the Teacher: Collect sample brochures from a travel agency so students have models.

Olympic Summer Games Jigsaw

Directions: Cut out the pieces on pages 30–32 and match them together to find out about some of the Olympic Summer sports. Each puzzle has three pieces.

Olympic Summer Games Jigsaw *(cont.)*

Directions: Cut out the pieces on pages 30–32 and match them together to find out about some of the Olympic Summer sports. Each puzzle has three pieces.

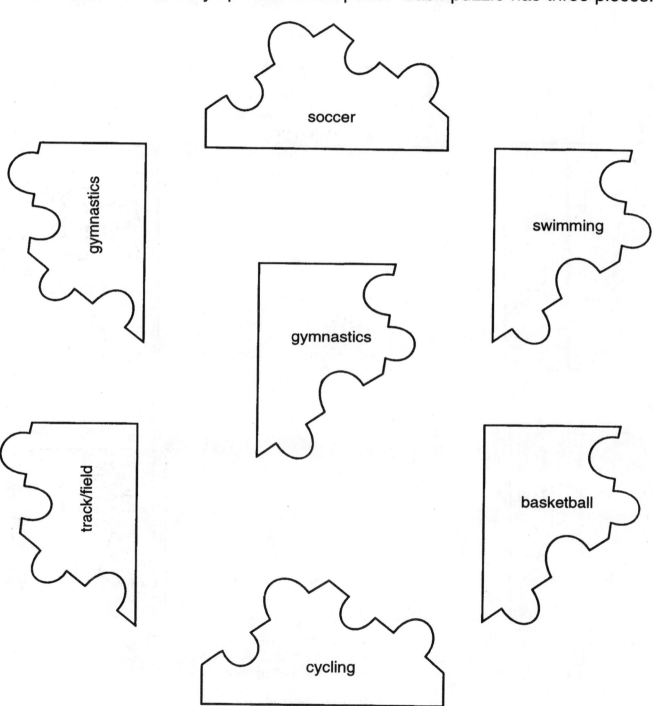

Olympic Summer Games Jigsaw *(cont.)*

Directions: Cut out the pieces on pages 30–32 and match them together to find out about some of the Olympic Summer events. Each puzzle has three pieces.

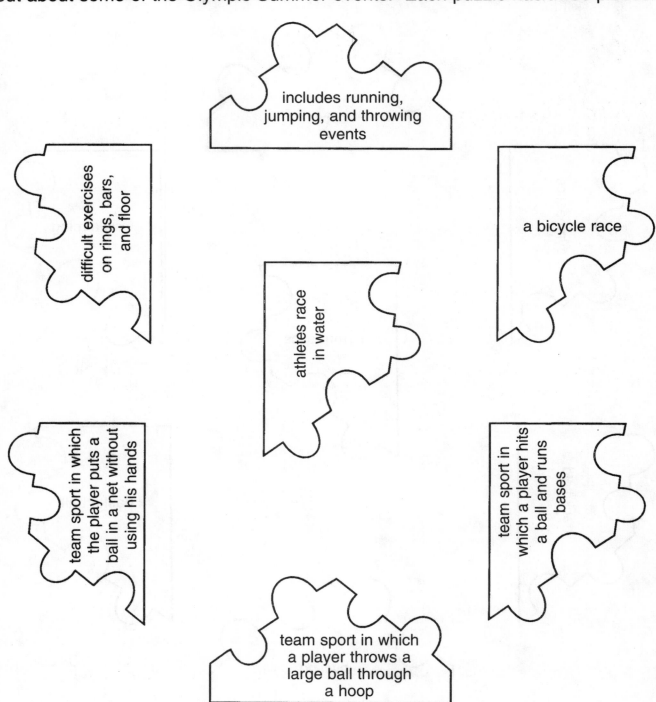

Olympic Winter Games Jigsaw

Directions: Cut out the pieces on pages 33–35 and match them together to find out about some of the Olympic Winter sports. Each puzzle has three pieces.

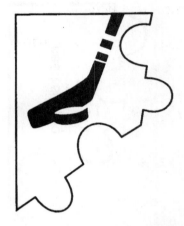

OlympicWinter
Games Jigsaw *(cont.)*

Directions: Cut out the pieces on pages 33–35 and match them together to find out about some of the Olympic Winter events. Each puzzle has three pieces.

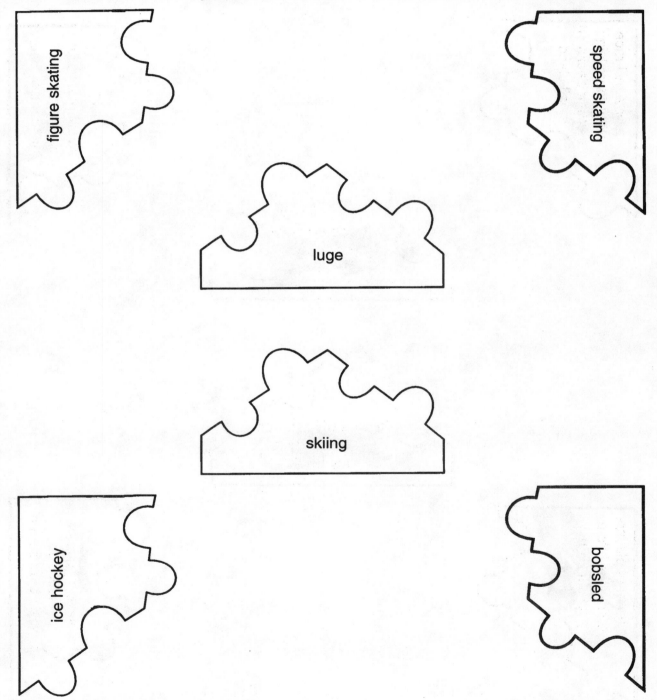

figure skating

speed skating

luge

skiing

ice hockey

bobsled

Olympic Winter Games Jigsaw *(cont.)*

Directions: Cut out the pieces on pages 33–35 and match them together to find out about some of the Olympic Winter sports. Each puzzle has three pieces.

a downhill race with riders lying on their backs on small sleds

men, women, and pairs do difficult spins and jumps

a race on snow for people wearing skis

teams of men ride a sled down an icy track

a team of players on skates hits a puck into a net

a race on a track for people wearing skates

Olympic Crossword Puzzle

Directions: Read the clues and then fill in the puzzle with words that have an **er** ending. Then answer the questions below.

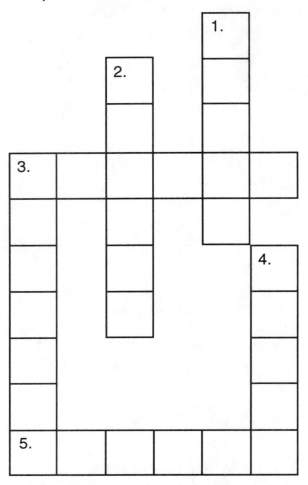

Across

3. A person who skates
5. A person who runs

Down

1. A person who dives
2. A person who plays
3. A person who swims
4. A person who skis

Which words have a double consonant before the "er"?

_____

_____

Is the vowel sound long or short in those words?

_____

Marathon

The marathon is a 26.2 mile (42 km) foot race. It is held on the last day of the Olympic Games. The race is run on a road and finishes at the same time as the closing ceremony. The runners come into a stadium full of cheering well-wishers.

In 490 B.C. a Grecian man named Pheidippides ran from Marathon to Athens, to report the defeat of the Persian army by the Greeks. This victory took place on the plain of Marathon. The distance between Athens and Marathon is about 25 miles (40 km).

How do you think runners would prepare to run a marathon?

- What foods would they eat?
- How much sleep would they need?
- How would they practice?
- What would they wear for the run?
- How might weather affect a runner?

Multi-Event Sports

Many Olympic sports have more than one part or contest. The Greek word "athlon" means contest. Count the contests below. Add "athlon" to the prefixes to name the events.

bi = 2   tri = 3   penta = 5   hepta = 7   deca = 10

1. Cross country skiing and shooting _____

2. Horseback riding, fencing, pistol shooting, swimming, and running _____

3. 100-meter hurdles, shot put, high jump, long jump, javelin, 800-meter race, and 200-meter race _____

4. High jump, high hurdles, shot put, 1,500-meter race,100-meter race, long jump, discus throw, pole vault, javelin, and 400-meter race _____

5. Swimming, biking, and running _____

Create a new sport with two or more events.

Name of the contest:_____

Name of events: _____

Where would you hold your contest?

_____

_____

_____

_____

How would you choose the competitors?

_____

_____

_____

_____

Event Analogies

Directions: Complete the sentences by using the words in the word bank.

1. A ball is to baseball as a ___ ___ ___ ___ is to hockey.

2. A net is to soccer as a ___ ___ ___ ___ is to basketball.

3. Sit is to bobsled as ___ ___ ___ is to luge.

4. A skate is to a skater as a ___ ___ ___ is to a skier.

5. Pentathlon is to five as ___ ___ ___ ___ ___ ___ ___ ___ ___ is to ten.

6. A mat is to a gymnast as a ___ ___ ___ ___ is to a swimmer.

7. A stick is to hockey as a ___ ___ ___ is to baseball.

8. A bicycle is to a cyclist as a ___ ___ ___ ___ is to a bobber.

9. A crown of olive leaves is to the ancient Olympic Games as a ___ ___ ___ ___ ___ is to the Modern Games.

10. The Valley of Olympia is to the ancient Olympic Games as ___ ___ ___ ___ ___ ___ is to the Modern Games.

Word Bank: Athens   medal   bat   ski   pool
decathlon   lie   sled   hoop   puck

Event Report Form

Directions: Watch one event during the Olympic Games and then complete this form.

Name of the sport_____

When did you see the event?_____

Who participated? (circle one)   men   women

    Athletes' names _____

               _____

What did the athletes do?_____

How were they dressed? _____

      Name the winners:

          Gold medal_____

               Country_____

         Silver medal _____

               Country_____

        Bronze medal_____

               Country_____

Describe the awards ceremony. How do you think it would feel to win an Olympic medal?

_____

_____

_____

On the back of this or a separate piece of paper, draw a picture of an athlete receiving a medal or competing in the sport you watched.

What Is a Competitor?

Some people enjoy running for fun and exercise. They do not want to run in a race. These people are not competitors.

Some people enjoy racing other runners to see who can go the fastest. They like to win awards and medals. These people are called competitors.

People can compete in many ways. They like to enter science fairs, spelling bees, and art contests.

Are you a competitor? _____ (yes or no)

Explain your answer._____

_____

_____

What ways can you compete at school? _____

_____

_____

Do you play on a sports team? _____ (yes or no)

How do you feel after your team wins? _____

_____

_____

How do you feel after your team loses?_____

_____

_____

Is it good or bad to be a competitor? Explain._____

_____

_____

_____

Win or Lose? Journal

Pretend that you are an athlete at the Olympic Games. You could become a star or you might be a runner-up. What if you win a medal? What if you don't?

1. Write an entry for your journal, telling how you feel before the event.

2. Give as many details as you can about the competition.

3. Congratulations! You are a winner! Write another journal entry telling how you feel as the medal is placed around your neck.

4. Suppose you did not win an Olympic medal? Write a journal entry telling your feelings.

Design a cereal box with your picture on it.

Design a piece of athletic equipment (shoes, ball) that you would advertise.

Olympians and Sports

Note to the Teacher: Cut the cards along the dotted lines on the next five pages, laminate them, and use them as task cards at your Olympic Learning Center.

Basketball

Basketball was invented in 1891 by Dr. James Naismith, a physical education teacher. The first game used a round ball and two peach baskets as goals. In the beginning there were no free throws or dribbling.

The first professional game was played in Trenton, New Jersey, in 1896. Men's basketball became an Olympic sport in 1936. Women's basketball was added as a medal sport in 1976.

The United States "Dream Team," made up of professional basketball players, played in the Olympic Games in 1992.

Answer the following:

1. When did women's basketball become an Olympic sport?
2. Make a list of the 1992 "Dream Team" players.

To do:

On a separate piece of paper, draw a diagram of a basketball court, showing the free-throw lines and three-point field goal lines. Also add the backboards to your picture.

Michael Jordan

(1963–   )

Michael Jeffrey Jordan was born February 17, 1963, in Wallace, North Carolina. He liked to play basketball against his brother Larry in their backyard.

Michael knew he had to work hard to build his basketball skills. He turned professional after his junior year in college. Today, Michael plays for the Chicago Bulls.

Michael played on the United States Olympic basketball teams and won gold medals in 1984 and 1992.

Answer the following:

1. When and where was Michael Jordan born?
2. What players besides Michael were on the 1992 USA Olympic basketball team?
3. How did Michae! build his basketball skills?

Olympians and Sports *(cont.)*

Figure Skating

An American named Jackson Haines added ballet, music, and colorful costumes to the sport of ice skating.

Figure skating became an Olympic event in 1908. The skaters must perform difficult moves, jumps, and spins.

Pair skating began in Vienna, Austria, in the 1880s. The partners perform difficult throws and lifts.

Ice dancing became an Olympic sport in 1976.

Answer the following:

    1. How is figure skating different from speed skating?

To do:

On a separate piece of paper, draw a figure skater in costume. Suggest some music to go with the costume.

Scott Hamilton

(1958–   )

Scott Hamilton was born August 28, 1958, in Toledo, Ohio. At age two, he became very ill. His body could not use food to help him grow.

Hamilton began figure skating. A year later, his doctor said he was healthy. The exercise and cold air at the rink had made him well.

Hamilton began working harder than ever on his skating. He went to the 1980 Winter Olympic Games. Hamilton was able to make the most difficult jumps and spins look easy.

He won a gold medal at the Olympic Winter Games in 1984. Hamilton travels and performs with *Stars on Ice*. He is also on television during Olympic figure skating events.

Answer the following:

    1. How has hard work helped Scott Hamilton?

    2. Does Hamilton still enjoy skating? How do you know?

Olympians and Sports *(cont.)*

Gymnastics

Friedrich Ludwig Jahn, a German, is the father of modern gymnastics. He invented the parallel bars, horizontal bar, balance beam, horse, and the rings.

Gymnastics is an enjoyable sport to watch. Gymnasts compete as a team and as individuals. Sometimes the athletes do especially difficult moves to earn extra points. The highest possible score is a 10.

Men's gymnastics became an Olympic sport in 1896. Women's gymnastics became an Olympic sport in 1928. The sport of rhythmic gymnastics was added to the Summer Olympic Games in 1984 for women.

To do:

- On a separate piece of paper, draw parallel bars, a horizontal bar, a balance beam, a horse, and rings.
- How do men's, women's, and rhythmic gymnastics differ?

Nadia Comaneci

(1961–   )

Nadia Comaneci was born November 12, 1961, in Onesti, Romania. She was six years old when Bela Karolyi saw her playing on the school grounds. He was the coach of the Romanian Olympic gymnastics team.

Her parents agreed to let Nadia go to a special school for training. Nadia was a perfect student. She did not get tired of doing the same exercises over and over.

Nadia was a member of the 1976 Romanian Olympic team. She scored seven perfect 10s and received one bronze, one silver, and three gold medals.

Answer the following:

1. What was Nadia Comaneci's greatest gymnastic achievement?
2. What made Nadia a perfect student?
3. Who is Bela Karolyi? What is he doing today?

Olympians and Sports *(cont.)*

Track and Field

Track and field events began with a short race at the first modern Olympic Games. Other events, like the javelin, discus, and long jump, were added later.

Great athletes like Babe Didrikson, Jesse Owens, and Carl Lewis have helped to make track and field popular all around the world.

Track events include all foot races. Field events include jumping and throwing. The events are held on outside tracks.

Answer the following:

1. Name three famous track and field athletes.
2. What are track events? What are field events?
3. List the Olympic events in track and field.

Carl Lewis

(1961–   )

Frederick Carlton Lewis was born on July 1, 1961, in Birmingham, Alabama. His parents were high school track coaches.

Carl became interested in track after meeting Jesse Owens in 1971. He worked out with his parents and two years later was the best high school track athlete in the United States.

Lewis won four gold medals in the 1984 Summer Olympic Games for three races and the long jump. He won two gold medals and one silver medal in the 1988 Summer Olympic Games.

In 1992, Carl won two more Olympic gold medals in the long jump and 400-meter relay race. His final gold medal came in the long jump at the 1996 Atlanta Summer Olympic Games.

Answer the following:

1. How did Carl's parents help him as an athlete?
2. How many gold medals does Carl Lewis have?

Olympians and Sports *(cont.)*

Baseball

The first baseball game was held in Hoboken, New Jersey, in 1846. There were two teams of nine players. The men hit a ball with a bat and ran around bases to score points.

Millions of people around the world attend baseball games each year. There are two professional major leagues in the United States. The best team is decided at the World Series in October.

Baseball was made a medal sport in the Summer Olympic Games of 1992.

To do:

- Create a baseball card for your favorite player.
- Draw a diagram of a baseball diamond, marking each of the players' positions. What equipment does each player use?

Jim Abbott

(1967–   )

Jim Abbott loved baseball, but he was born with a right arm that ended at the wrist. He has no right hand.

Jim practiced every day to become a good left-handed pitcher. He held his glove on the end of his right arm and switched it to his left hand to catch balls.

In high school, Jim was a star athlete. He won a scholarship to play baseball for the University of Michigan.

In the 1988 Summer Olympic Games he was the winning pitcher in the final game against Japan. Later, Jim Abbott became a professional baseball player. He pitched a no-hitter on September 4, 1993, for the New York Yankees.

Answer the following:

1. Name three of Jim's achievements in baseball after high school.
2. How can a handicap have a positive effect on a person?

Olympic Dream Teams Book

To the Teacher:

- Have students design a book cover from a 9" x 12" (23 cm x 30 cm) piece of construction paper.

- Make a book with five pieces of drawing paper (one for each team).

- Organize the book with a drawing page behind each printed page. Staple on the left. Students can add an illustration for each "Dream Team."

- If you wish, prepare another half page (for creative writing or research) to include at the end of the book, using the pattern below.

1980 Hockey

Team U.S.A. was made up of young college players. Their coach was Herb Brooks. The team went to Lake Placid dreaming of a gold medal, but many people did not believe in them.

They began the tournament with a win against Sweden. Next they won the game against Czechoslovakia. The third game was against the Soviet Union, a team that had won four Olympic gold medals. They played a rough game, but the Americans got the win.

In the final game, Team U.S.A. beat Finland. It seemed that the whole country cheered as Mike Eruzione accepted the gold medal for his team. America got a chance to believe in miracles.

Olympic Dream Teams Book *(cont.)*

1936 Track and Field

The U.S. track and field team went to compete in Germany when Adolf Hitler was in power. He believed white Germans were the best athletes in every sport.

The most famous member of the U.S. team was Jesse Owens, a black man. He won four gold medals and set two Olympic records.

The rest of that U.S. team did well too. They won gold medals in the 400-meter run and the 110-meter hurdles and silver medals in the 800- and 1500-meter runs. They won three medals in the high jump and two in the discus throw. The team also took all three medals in the two-day decathlon.

The victories of the 1936 U.S. team were the most remarkable in Olympic track and field history.

1976 Boxing

The U.S. boxing team won 35 of 41 bouts in the 1976 Olympics. They brought home five gold medals, one silver, and one bronze.

The boxers had a good coach, Pat Nappi. He taught them to move toward their opponents and punch from side to side. European boxers couldn't fight this way. The American boxers were fast and strong, and they fought hard to win.

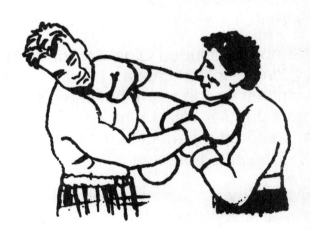

The best remembered boxer from the 1976 team is Sugar Ray Leonard. Several of the team members went on to be successful professional boxers.

Olympic Dream Teams Book *(cont.)*

1960 Basketball

The men on the U.S. Olympic basketball team were talented individuals. Their coach, Pete Newell, had to teach them to play well together. He knew teamwork would win the gold medal.

The 1960 Olympics were held in Rome, and the U.S. team played the first game of the semifinals against the Italian team. The fans cheered for the home team, but the Italians could not overcome the powerful Americans. The game was a rough one with 71 fouls, but the final score was United States, 112 and Italy, 81.

Even the Brazilian team was no match for the Americans in the gold medal game. The final score was United States, 90 and Brazil, 63.

1976 Gymnastics

The same year that Nadia Comaneci (of Romania) was the best individual gymnast in the world, the Soviet Union had the best women's team in the world.

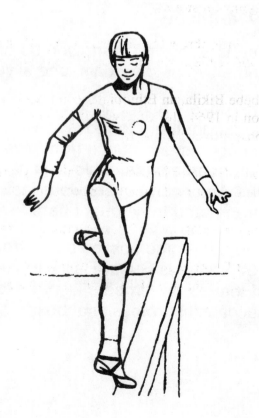

Members included Olga Korbut, Nelli Kim, and Lyudmila Tourishcheva. Lyudmila was the best gymnast on the team, but Olga Korbut was the most popular. Nelli Kim won two gold medals and scored a perfect 10 on the floor exercise and the side horse vault.

Every Soviet team member was in the top 10 overall. They won the team combined gold medal.

Olympic Trivia

Here are some interesting and unusual stories about past Olympic athletes to share with your students.

Wilma Rudolph had scarlet fever and pneumonia as a young child. For a time she could not walk, but with her family's help and lots of hard work and determination, Wilma made the U.S. Olympic track team. In the 1956 Olympic Summer Games she won two bronze medals, and in the 1960 Olympic Summer Games she won three gold medals in track.

Jim Abbott loved baseball so much that he learned to pitch and bat left-handed. The fact that he had no right hand was a fact he learned to work around. He won a scholarship to the University of Michigan and won many pitching honors. In the 1988 Olympics he pitched the final game against Japan to clinch the gold medal for the USA.

Joan Benoit Samuelson became the first women to win an Olympic marathon in 1984, having had knee surgery just seventeen days before the Olympic Trials.

Greg Louganis is the first man to win gold medals in both diving events in two successive Olympic Games (1984 and 1988).

Mark Spitz won a record seven gold medals in swimming events at the 1972 Games. He had previously won two gold medals, as well as bronze and silver medals at the 1968 Olympic Summer Games.

Speed skater Bonnie Blair won five gold medals in 1994, the most won by any American woman in Olympic history.

Al Oerter threw the discus to win gold medals in four successive Olympic Summer Games (1956–1968). He set a new Olympic record each time.

Abebe Bikila, an Ethiopian, won the marathon in 1960, running without shoes. He ran it again and won in 1964, this time wearing shoes. He is the only man in Olympic history to have won two consecutive marathons.

Sonja Henie of Norway was only 19 years old when she appeared in her first Olympic Winter Games. She did not medal that year but went on to win three gold medals in 1928, 1932, and 1936.

Connie Paraskevin-Young is a medalist in both cycling and speed skating.

Janet Evans, America's top woman swimmer, won three gold medals in the 1988 Olympic Summer Games at the age of 17. She also won gold in 1992.

Postcard

Directions: Pretend you are an Olympic athlete. Write a postcard to a friend or family member. Cut out the postcard and draw a picture of the host city on the front.

Olympic Products

Sometimes Olympic athletes need a quick snack. Pretend you are in the fast food business and create a snack that would be healthy for athletes who need lots of energy.

Draw your ideas here.

. . . .

Olympic athletes often use special equipment and products to make them more comfortable or help them perform better. Pretend you are a weary athlete and create one product which would make you feel or perform better.

Draw your ideas here.

Word Search Puzzle

```
L  L  A  B  T  E  K  S  A  B  Y  G  C
F  I  G  U  R  E  S  K  A  T  I  N  G
C  B  Y  N  I  S  W  P  J  O  B  I  K
E  T  M  E  S  K  I  I  N  G  O  T  D
H  Q  N  Z  O  D  M  M  T  F  B  A  I
O  R  A  V  C  H  M  F  I  Y  S  K  V
J  G  S  T  C  U  I  O  R  M  L  S  I
H  O  T  W  E  N  N  I  K  T  E  D  N
L  B  I  N  R  J  G  O  P  G  D  E  G
Y  S  C  T  M  I  O  M  U  X  V  E  L
B  A  S  E  B  A  L  L  Y  D  R  P  M
Q  W  C  Y  C  L  I  N  G  H  I  S  K
T  R  A  C  K  A  N  D  F  I  E  L  D
O  J  L  B  Y  E  K  C  O  H  E  C  I
```

Directions: Circle the summer sports in one color and the winter sports in another.

Winter Sports
figure skating
ice hockey
skiing
speed skating
bobsled
luge

Summer Sports
gymnastics
swimming
diving
baseball
basketball
cycling
soccer
track and field

Design an Official Uniform

Directions: Each country has a special uniform, often a warm-up suit. Design an official warmup suit for an Olympic athlete.

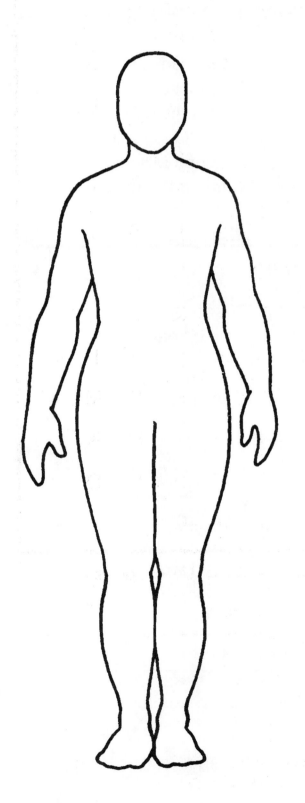 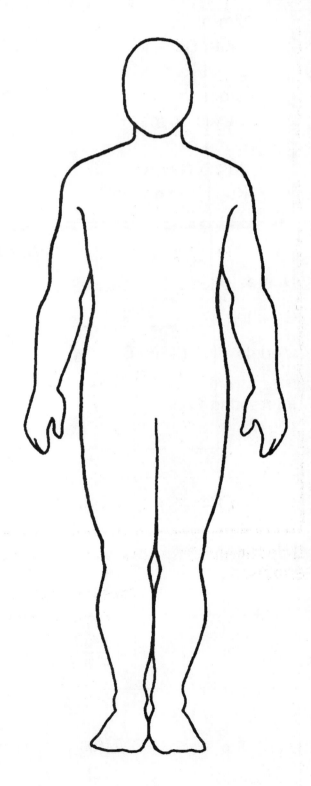

Olympian Report Form

Directions: Choose one of the Olympic stars below. Then use a reference book to complete a report.

Jim Abbott	Abebe Bikila	Bonnie Blair
Brian Boitano	Nadia Comaneci	Babe Didrikson
Janet Evans	Sonja Henie	Dan Jansen
Bruce Jenner	Michael Jordan	Florence Griffith Joyner
Jackie Joyner-Kersee	Nancy Kerrigan	Jean Claude Killy
Carl Lewis	Greg Louganis	Shannon Miller
Jesse Owens	Mary Lou Retton	Katerina Witt
Kristi Yamaguchi		

Famous Olympian

Name: _____ Sport:_____

Country: _____ Olympic Year(s):_____

Medals Won (if any):_____

Interesting Facts:

1. _____

2. _____

3. _____

If I could meet _____, I would ask him/her
(athlete's name)

_____

_____

_____

This Is My Country

Pretend you are an Olympic athlete from another country. Answer these questions to share information about your country with another athlete.

My country is_____

Here is its flag.

My country is located in _____

The capital city is _____

The weather is _____ in summer

and _____ in winter.

My country has (circle)

    rivers   rain forests   mountains   volcanos   wildlife

Our farmers grow _____

We enjoy eating _____

Our favorite holidays are_____

People visit my country to see _____

_____

The ABCs of the Olympics

Directions: Think about all you have learned about the Olympic Games. Print a word on the lines for each letter of the alphabet.

You may use names of athletes, cities, equipment, or sports.

A _____   N _____

B _____   O _____

C _____   P _____

D _____   Q _____

E _____   R _____

F _____   S _____

G _____   T _____

H _____   U _____

I _____   V _____

J _____   W _____

K _____   X _____

L _____   Y _____

M _____   Z _____

Use your list to make a flap book or chart.

- Make a small picture of each word.

- Cut another paper big enough to cover the picture.

- Glue it to the page (or chart paper) along one side.

- Print the letter on the flap.

- Be sure the pages or (pictures) are in ABC order.

- Bind your pages in a cover or display your chart for other students to enjoy.

Road to the Olympic Games

This is a game for three players. Each one will earn a "medal."

Preparation:

- Copy and construct the game board (pages 62 and 63). The game will start in Athens, Greece. You will need to add the location of the next Olympic Games at the finish line.

- Mount the game board on a file folder.

- Laminate the board, if possible.

- Copy and cut apart the questions (pages 60 and 61).

- Provide three game markers.

- Prepare a supply of "medals." Cut yellow, white, and tan construction paper into medal or ribbon shapes. Mark the yellow "1st," white "2nd," and tan "3rd."

How to Play:

You will move along the path from the first Olympic Games to the upcoming Olympic Games. Follow the directions on the game board.

Put the question cards face down in a pile. The first player reads the top card to the student on his right. If the question is answered correctly, he moves along the path. The next player takes a card and repeats the process. If a player cannot answer, he/she loses a turn. Play continues until everyone reaches the finish line.

The first player to the finish line moves his/her marker to "1" position on the podium. He/she is the gold medal winner. The second player to the finish line moves his/her marker to the "2" on the podium and receives a silver medal. The third player to finish moves his/her marker to the "3" position on the podium and receives a bronze medal.

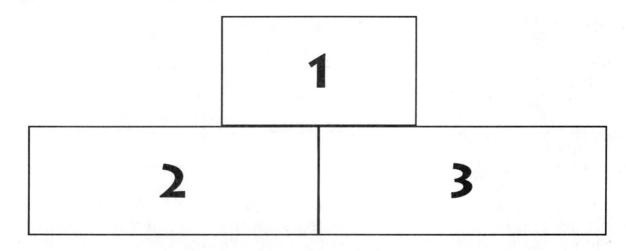

Road to the Olympic Games *(cont.)*

Directions: Cut apart the cards, match them to the answers on page 61, and then glue or tape them back to back.

1. In what country did the Olympics begin?	2. How many years are there between the summer and winter Olympic Games?	3. Who participated in the ancient Olympic Games?
4. What is the prize for first place at the Olympic Games?	5. What is the prize for third place at the Olympic Games?	6. What is a chariot?
7. In what year did the modern Olympics begin?	8. In what year did the ancient Olympics begin?	9. What is used to light the Olympic flame?
10. What are the colors of the five Olympic rings?	11. What do the rings stand for?	12. Which country's team is the first to walk in the opening ceremonies?
13. In what order do the athletes enter the opening ceremonies?	14. Who carries the flag of each team into the stadium?	15. What animal was the first Olympic mascot?
16. What must a city have to host the Winter Games?	17. Name three cities in the United States that have hosted the Olympics.	18. What is the longest race in the Olympics?
19. Which Olympic Games has more events, summer or winter?	20. Name three sports played on ice.	21. What is Jim Abbott's sport?
22. What was Carl Lewis' sport?	23. What was Nadia Comaneci's sport?	24. What is Michael Jordan's sport?

Road to the Olympic Games (cont.)

Directions: Cut apart the cards, match them to the questions on page 60, and then glue or tape them back to back.

1. Greece Move ahead 1 space.	2. two Move ahead 1 space.	3. men and boys Move ahead 1 space.
4. gold medal Move ahead 1 space.	5. bronze medal Move ahead 1 space.	6. A two-wheeled carriage pulled by four horses. Move ahead 3 spaces.
7. 1896 Move ahead 3 spaces.	8. 776 B.C. Move ahead 3 spaces.	9. Olympic torch Move ahead 1 space.
10. red, blue, black, yellow, and green Move ahead 5 spaces.	11. six continents Move ahead 1 space.	12. Greece Move ahead 1 space.
13. alphabetical order Move ahead 3 spaces.	14. An athlete chosen by his/her team. Move ahead 3 spaces.	15. a dog Move ahead 1 space.
16. snow Move ahead 1 space.	17. Atlanta, Los Angeles, Lake Placid Move ahead 5 spaces.	18. the marathon Move ahead 1 space.
19. summer Move ahead 1 space.	20. speed skating, figure skating, and ice hockey Move ahead 3 spaces.	21. baseball Move ahead 1 space.
22. track and field Move ahead 1 space.	23. gymnastics Move ahead 1 space.	24. basketball Move ahead 1 space.

Road to the Olympic Games *(cont.)*

You're a Champ! Take an extra turn		
		You need more practice. Lose 1 turn.

ATHENS GREECE

Road to the Olympic Games *(cont.)*

You need more practice. Lose 1 turn.

You're a Champ! Take an extra turn

| 1 |
| 2 | 3 |

NEXT OLYMPICS

A Mini-Olympics

Your students will have fun staging their own "mini" Olympics. Here are some suggestions.

Have your students help in measuring the area. Making metric and standard measurement comparisons is a good math activity.

Planning the Games

Choose four track and field events:

50-Meter Dash: Athletes will run on a measured track.

4 x 50-Meter Relay: A team of four runners will pass a baton while running on a measured track.

Discus Throw: Athletes will throw a frisbee for distance.

Long Jump: A measured jump from a standing position, it is best done on grass or sand.

All students should sign up to participate in one event. Ask an older student(s) to help with timing races and measuring jumps and throws.

Scheduling the Games

Here is a sample schedule. You may find it necessary to ask your physical education teacher to help with preliminaries.

Prelims

Girls' Events

1. Girls' 50m Dash—9:00 a.m.
3. Girls' Relay—9:40 a.m.
5. Girls' Discus—10:20 a.m.
7. Girls' Long Jump—11:00 a.m.

Boys' Events

2. Boys' 50m Dash—9:20 a.m.
4. Boys' Relay—10:00 a.m.
6. Boys' Discus—10:40 a.m.
8. Boys' Long Jump—11:20 a.m.

Finals

Girls' 50m Dash—11:30 a.m.
Girls' Relay—11:50 p.m.
Girls' Discus—12:15 p.m.
Girls' Long Jump—12:45p.m.

Boys' 50m Dash—11:40 a.m.
Boys' Relay—12:00 p.m.
Boys' Discus—12:30 p.m.
Boys' Long Jump—1:00p.m.

A Mini-Olympics *(cont.)*

Organizing the Games

50-Meter Dash—For the most accurate results, each runner will have to run and be timed individually. Use a stopwatch to determine the times. If you do not have a stopwatch, you may start all the runners at the same time and make a visual judgement about the first four finishers. They will advance to the finals.

Relay Race—Assign runners to teams of four and explain that they must pass a baton (an unsharpened pencil) to the next runner as they cross the finish line. Watch carefully to determine the first four teams to finish. They will advance to the finals.

Discus Throw—Each participant may have three tries to throw a frisbee. Use helpers to mark the distances, keeping only the best attempt. The four players with the longest throws will advance to the finals.

Long Jump—Each participant may have three tries to jump from a marked starting line. Use helpers to measure the jumps with a tape or meter stick. Record only the longest jump. If a player falls backwards, disqualify that attempt. The four players with the longest jumps will advance to the finals.

Certificates and Medals

Each participant should receive a certificate (page 66). You may add self-sticking seals in gold, silver, and bronze to the certificates of the three finalists or have students use the patterns on page 19 to design medals which can be hung around the neck from a ribbon.

Performance Certificate

Proud Participant in Mini-Olympics

Student's Name

Teacher/Coach

Date

Olympic Display

Students can use these pictures to design a large freestanding display or in dioramas of individual sports.

You will need the following:

- patterns, pages 72–76

- lightweight tagboard

- scissors

- stapler

- glue stick

- crayons or markers

- construction paper scraps

- shoe box (optional)

Directions:

1. Color the individual pictures.

2. Mount them on lightweight tagboard and cut around the shapes.

3. Bend the bottom strip into a circle and staple it closed so that the figure will stand. (Staple A to B.)

4. Design the appropriate scenery and/or equipment from construction paper.

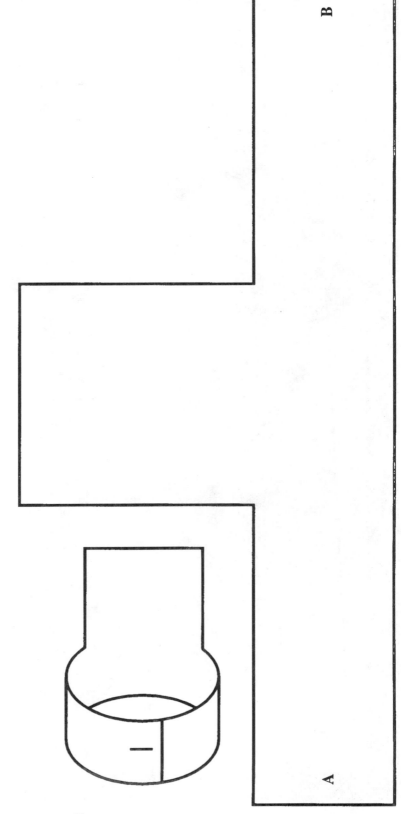

World Map

World Map *(cont.)*

Additional Activities and Enrichment

Use your imagination and creativity to extend the Olympic experience to all areas of the curriculum. Encourage your students to do the following:

- Keep an Olympic diary. They can record the events they watched each day or list medal winners.

- Make a classroom chart for two or three favorite sports. Indicate participating athletes names, events, and nationalities.

- Make a large time line showing dates and picturing highlights of each Olympic Games.

- Locate and label host cities on a map of the world.

- Write letters to their favorite athletes. Send them to:

   The U.S. Olympic Committee

   Colorado Springs, Colorado 80906

- Make a trading card of your favorite Olympic athlete.

- Write the rules for your favorite Olympic event.

- Make measurements on the playground to indicate the distance of the 100-meter run.

- Practice measuring your students' long jumps.

- Practice using a stopwatch for timed races.

- Create an Olympic souvenir store (or catalog) with items and prices indicated. Students can practice counting and making change.

- Relate animals to the sport to which they are best adapted (e.g., monkeys/gymnastics, cheetah/track and field, etc.).

- Discuss the importance of a healthful diet to an athlete in training.

- Create an Olympic flag.

Additional Activities and Enrichment *(cont.)*

Science Suggestions

Winter Olympic Games

Use this experiment to help your students understand that friction and resistance are lower on an ice-covered surface.

You will need the following:

- a 9" x 13" (23 cm x 33 cm) cake pan
- water
- freezer
- books about 3" x 4" (8 cm x 10 cm) thick
- 12" x 18" (30 cm x 40 cm) carpet square
- several common items made of different materials: penny, marble, pencil, blackboard eraser, heavy rubber bands wrapped around a block of wood

Directions:

1. Freeze about 1" (2.5 cm) of water in the bottom of the cake pan.
2. Create an incline for the pan and the carpet square, using the books.
3. Predict and compare the times necessary for each item to slide down the two surfaces.

Summer Olympic Games

Use this experiment to help your students understand that objects will react differently when striking a hard surface.

You will need the following:

- a basketball, baseball, soccer ball, volleyball (optional)
- yardstick

Directions:

1. Predict how high each ball will bounce when dropped from a specific height. Drop all three balls from the same height. Record the height of the first bounce for each ball. Compare your predictions with the actual bounces.

2. Predict how many times each ball will bounce when dropped from a specific height. Drop all three balls from the same height. Record the number of bounces for each ball. Compare your predictions with the actual number of bounces.

3. Draw conclusions about how the size and weight of the ball affects its bounce.

Pictograms

Winter

BIATHLON

BOBSLED

FIGURE SKATING

ICE HOCKEY

LUGE

SKIING

Pictograms *(cont.)*

SPEED SKATING

Summer

ARCHERY

ATHLETICS

BASEBALL

BASKETBALL

Pictograms *(cont.)*

BOXING

CANOE/KAYAK

CYCLING

DIVING

EQUESTRAIN

GYMNASTICS

Pictograms *(cont.)*

MODERN PENTATHLON

ROWING

SHOOTING

SOCCER

SOFTBALL

SWIMMING

Pictograms *(cont.)*

SYNCHRONIZED SWIMMING

TAEKWANDO

TENNIS

VOLLEYBALL

WATER POLO

WRESTLING

Answer Key

Modern Games Sort (page 11)

Sports in Water—swimming, diving

Sports on Ice/Snow—figure skating, speed skating, skiing, bobsled, luge, ice hockey

Sports Using a Ball—baseball, basketball, soccer

Sports on a Track—cycling, speed skating, track and field

Olympics Crossword Puzzle (page 36)

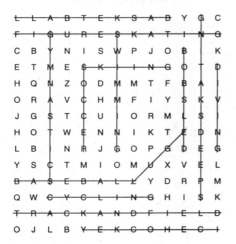

Multi-Event Sports (page 38)

Answers: 1. biathlon, 2. pentathlon, 3. heptathlon, 4. decathlon, 5. triathlon

Event Analogies (page 39)

Answers: 1. puck, 2. hoop, 3. lie, 4. ski, 5. decathlon, 6. pool, 7. bat, 8. sled, 9. medal, 10. Athens

Word Search Puzzle (page 54)

Bibliography

ACOG. *Official Commemorative Book Atlanta '96.* Woodford, 1996.

Anderson, Dave. *The Story of Basketball.* Morrow, 1988.

Arnold, Caroline. *The Summer Olympics.* Franklin Watts, 1991.
   Olympic Winter Games. Franklin Watts, 1991.

Bailey, Donna. *Cycling.* Raintree, 1990.

Baker, William J. *Jesse Owens: An American Life.* The Free Press, 1986.

Barry, James P. *The Berlin Olympics, 1936: Black American Athletics Counter Nazi Propaganda.* Franklin Watts, 1975.

Benson, Michael. *Dream Teams.* Little, Brown, 1991.

Birenbaum, Barbara. *Olympic Glow.* Peartree, 1990.

Bloom, Marc. *Basketball.* Scholastic, 1991.

Braden, Vic and Louis Phillips. *Sportsathon.* Puffin, 1986.

Broklin, Yuri. *The Big Red Machine: The Rise and Fall of Soviet Olympic Champions.* Random House, 1978.

Carlson, Lewis H. and John J. Fogarty. *Tales of Gold.* Contemporary Books, 1987.

Carrier, Roch. *Boxing Champion.* Tundra Books, 1991.

Chester, David. *The Olympic Games Handbook: An Authentic History of Both the Ancient and Modern Olympic Games, Complete Results and Records.* Scribner, 1975.

Christesen, Barbara. *First Olympic Games.* Contemporary Perspectives, 1978.

Cohen, Daniel. *Wrestling Superstars.* Pocket, 1985.

Cohen, Neil. *The Everything You Want to Know about Sports Encyclopedia.* Sports Illustrated for Kids Book, 1994.

Coote, James. *A Picture History of the Olympics.* Macmillan, 1972.

Dershem, Kurt. *Olympians.* Iron Crown, 1990.

Devaney, John. *Great Olympic Champions.* Putnam, 1967.

Dieterich, Michelle. *Skiing.* Lerner Pub., 1992.

Dress, Ludwig. *Olympia: Gods, Artists, and Athletes.* Praeger, 1968.

Durant, John. *Highlights of the Olympics: From Ancient Times to the Present.* Hastings House, 1977.

Duden, Jane. *Olympics.* Macmillan Child Grp., 1991.

Duder, Tessa. *Journey to Olympia.* Scholastic, 1992.

Bibliography *(cont.)*

Evan, Jeremy. *Skiing.* Macmillan Child Grp., 1992.

Finlay, Moses I. and H.W. Pleket. *The Olympic Games: The First Thousand Years.* Viking Press, 1976.

Finlayson, Ann. *Stars of the Modern Olympics.* Garrard, 1967.

Frontier Press. *The Lincoln Library of Sports Champions*, (14 vols.). Frontier Press, 1993.

Hennessy, B. G. *Olympics!* Viking, 1996.

Hickok, Ralph. *The Encyclopedia of North American Sports History.* Facts on File, 1992.

IOC. *Official Olympic Companion.* Brassey's, 1996.

Knight, Theodore. *The Olympic Games.* Lucent, 1991.

Krebs, Gary M. (Editor). *The Guiness Book of Sports Records.* Running Press, 1989.

Kristy, Davida. *Coubertin's Olympics.* Lerner, 1995.

Miller, David. *Olympic Revolution*. Pavilion, 1996.

Ryan, Joan. *Little Girls in Pretty Boxes: the Making and Breaking of Elite Gymnasts and Figure Skaters.* Doubleday, 1995.

Salem Press. *Great Athletes of the Twentieth Century*, (23 vols.). Salem Press, 1992.

Sullivan, George. *Great Lives—Sports.* Scribner, 1988.

Tatlow, Peter. *The Olympics.* Bookwright Press, 1988.

USOC. *A Basic Guide to Archery.* Griffin Publishing, 1997.

USOC. *A Basic Guide to Cycling.* Griffin Publishing, 1997.

USOC. *A Basic Guide to Decathlon.* Griffin Publishing, 1996.

USOC. *A Basic Guide to Olympism.* Griffin Publishing, 1996.

USOC. *A Basic Guide to Equestrian.* Griffin Publishing, 1995.

USOC. *A Basic Guide to Soccer.* Griffin Publishing, 1995.

USOC. *Athens to Atlanta.* Commemorative, 1993.

USOC. *Atlanta 1996.* Commemorative, 1996.

USOC. *Chamonix to Lillehammer.* Mikko Laitinen, 1994.

USOC. *The 1984 Olympic Games.* Random House, ABC, 1984.

Walsh, John. *The Summer Olympics.* Franklin Watts, 1979.

Ward, Carl. *Hockey.* Sterling, 1991.

The Paralympic Games

The first Paralympic Games were held in Rome in 1960 and have been held every four years following the Olympic Games. The Paralympic Games have usually been held in the city or country hosting the Olympic Games. The vision for the events came from Dr. Ludwig Guttman of the Stoke-Mandeville Hospital in England. He worked with many veterans of World War II who suffered from spinal cord injuries. He dreamed of a world-class event to spotlight athletes with physical disabilities.

In 1988, the Paralympic Games were held immediately following the Olympic Games in Seoul, Korea, using the same Olympic facilities. In September 1992, again following the Olympic Games, Barcelona welcomed the athletes of the IXth Paralympiad. From opening and closing ceremonies to competitions in Olympic venues, the 1992 Paralympic Games mirrored the Olympic celebration held three weeks earlier.

Paralympic competitors will include athletes who are blind or visually impaired, paraplegics (whose legs are partially or totally paralyzed), quadriplegics (whose legs and arms are partially or totally paralyzed), people with cerebral palsy, amputees (who have had a limb partially or completely removed), dwarfs, and those with other disabilities. The athletes will be selected to represent their countries based on performances at qualifying events. There were more than 4,000 athletes at the 1996 Paralympic Games, representing 102 countries. Minor modifications are sometimes made to the rules of each sport to accommodate some of the athletes' disabilities. Athletes are classified according to severity of disability and compete against athletes with similar disabilities.

PARALYMPIC SPORTS PROGRAM

ARCHERY: Individual and team events; standing and wheelchair competitions with archers grouped in classes according to disability

ATHLETICS: Track, throwing and jumping events, cross-country, pentathlon and marathon

BASKETBALL: Played in wheelchairs by paraplegics, amputees and people with polio; few modifications to the rules; basically the same as the game played in the Olympic Games

BOCCIA: Similar to lawn bowling; played by athletes with a severe degree of cerebral palsy

CYCLING: Road racing using a variety of distances; three groups according to disability; cerebral palsy, visual impairment and impaired mobility

EQUESTRIAN: Focus on dressage events

FENCING: Foil, sabre and epee events; fencers compete in wheelchairs fastened to the floor

GOALBALL: Played by blind competitors; event uses balls containing bells to orient the athletes; object is to score goals that are located at either end of the playing field

JUDO: Visually impaired men follow International Judo Federation rules with only slight modifications

LAWN BOWLS: Similar to boccia, but played on a larger area; amputees, athletes with visual impairment and wheelchair athletes participate